THE WRITTEN CONSTITUTION AND THE UNWRITTEN ATTITUDE

THE WRITTEN CONSTITUTION AND THE UNWRITTEN ATTITUDE

BY

CHARLES EDWARD MERRIAM

Professor of Political Science in
The University of Chicago

LECTURES DELIVERED ON THE CUTLER FOUNDATION AT THE UNIVERSITY OF ROCHESTER, 1930

RICHARD R. SMITH, INC.
NEW YORK
1931

PRINTED IN THE UNITED STATES OF AMERICA
BY J. J. LITTLE & IVES COMPANY, NEW YORK

TO

MY SON

ROBERT

These lectures were given at the University of Rochester, New York, on March 19th, 20th and 21st, under the James C. Cutler Foundation. They are in no sense technical studies in the domain of public law, but represent the writer's convictions and experience in various fields traversed. The opinions expressed, it must of course be assumed, are those of the writer alone, and in no sense the conclusions of the University of Rochester or the Cutler Foundation.

CHARLES E. MERRIAM

CONTENTS

I

THE WRITTEN CONSTITUTION AND THE UNWRITTEN ATTITUDE

THE Constitution of the United States was one of the most revolutionary documents of its day—a shock to the sense of propriety in the established political and economic order of the time. The privileged few who sat upon comfortable thrones, if they really are comfortable, and drew their fat incomes from large landed estates, were horrified. Both throne and income depended on the principle of hereditary government and power combined—and they trembled at the thought of the complete abolition of the hereditary basis of power in the new government and the adoption of the elective principle. In those days the wealth of the time was in land; and land and political power went along together in the line of family descent. To break any link in this line was to break the chain that bound the government together. Outside of England the principle of the responsibility of the ruler to the ruled was political heresy of the first order, to be rigidly and ruthlessly repressed by all the coercive force of the law. And in Britain, birth was of prime importance.

I present the following propositions:

I. That the United States Constitution was revolutionary, experimental and adventurous in nature.

II. That many very fundamental changes in the basic features of our government have occurred under it.

III. That a constitution is in a sense a state of mind, and can be changed by changing our mind.

IV. That constitutional guaranties of person and property are slender and inadequate protection against the public will.

V. That the present danger in America is not that of lack of stability, but of mobility.

I. Our Constitution-makers were, when judged by the standards of their time, decided revolutionists. From the point of view of contemporary America, some have thought that the Constitution was conservative, or even reactionary in its tendencies; and in support of this position have cited some anti-democratic comments in the debates of the Constitutional Convention and some features of the new government such as the establishment of a powerful executive. President Wilson has commented upon this, in his *Division and Reunion* * (1893), "The Federal Government," said he, "was not by intention a democratic government. In plan and structure it had been meant to check the sweep and power of popular majorities."

Beard likewise, discussing the economic basis of the Constitution, found confirmation of Wilson's doctrine of the '90s.[1] J. A. Smith has contended in his well-known volume on *The Spirit of American Government* (1907) that the Constitution was framed in a reactionary spirit by conservatives who deliberately made the document difficult to amend, in order that propertied minorities might

* Pg. 12.

[1] *Economic Interpretation of the Constitution.*

be better protected.[2] I have commented on the swing away from the current of the earliest Revolutionary period, in my *History of American Political Theories,* but in writing my volume again, I should make the emphasis somewhat different.

If we look at the field from the world point of view, the Constitution was in reality a revolutionary document of the most disturbing character; and its makers were fully aware of this. They were willing to break with the old Articles of Confederation which provided for an unalterable union except with unanimous consent of all the states; to break with the world's political traditions; and to abandon the narrower precedents of the English establishment. They were ad-

[2] On this whole subject, see my *American Political Ideas,* Ch. VII, on "Democracy and Constitutional Change."

venturous, experimental, inventive, eager to adjust the forms and procedures of government to the actual forces and facts of their time. They were not unmindful of the business advantage of having a Constitution, but they were willing to work out this new government in terms of experiment and innovation.

Even more, they recognized that the Constitution they adopted was not perfect but must be changed from time to time, as conditions altered, and they made definite provision for amendment of the Constitution. Many of the contemporary American states made no such provision, and taking the world at large it was heresy to suggest the possibility of change in governments divinely established and ensured. That the Constitution was made difficult to amend was not due to the desire to prevent democratic change, but to the jealousy of the states, who feared the conditions they had exacted in a series of painful compromises might be swept away by a bare majority of their sister states, if unchecked by a requirement of an extraordinary majority. The important fact historically is not that amendment was made difficult, but that any provision was made for orderly change, and that nothing was excepted from change except the equal suffrage of the states in the senate, and one now forgotten provision regarding the slave trade.

The Constitution then was revolutionary in spirit, and in form provided for its own amendment and change with changing conditions. It was the work of political realists, who were undertaking an experiment, not writing a conclusion and a finality.

II. There have been many revolutionary changes under the Constitution. It is one of the commonest and most dangerous of errors to conclude that the Constitution of 1930 is really the same Constitution of 1789, or substantially so, and that any change in the Constitution is itself unconstitutional and undesirable. Many have asserted that the Constitution is too sacred to be touched; and in some states laws have even been passed making it criminal to advocate change in the form of the government, whether by violent means or by peaceful. But basic changes have been made in the actual constitution of government.

(1). The old balance of powers between state and nation has been revolutionized by courts and by civil war.

(2). The balance of power between legislative, executive and judiciary has been basically changed, to the advantage of the executive and the courts, while the congress has lost its original omnipotence.

(3). Political parties unmentioned in the Constitution direct and determine the course of public affairs.

(4). Slaves are free and women vote—developments incredible to the earlier generations. The terms and conditions of public life have been revolutionized since the days when gentlemen of substance and property ruled the land.

The truth is that each generation has produced a new constitution of government with fundamental changes in spirit and in form. The first generation saw the adoption of the party system which was not contemplated by the Constitution at all, and which nullified the provisions of the founders for the choice of president of the United States through the electoral college; and the rise of executive authority, undreamed of by the Founders. The next generation saw the upset of the balance between state and nation, first by judicial decision and then by civil war; and made basic changes regarding slavery and negro suffrage. The next period further developed a new executive power in the president, further disturbed the balance of power between states and the United States, revolutionized the electorate through the grant of women's suffrage, and in the Eighteenth Amendment undertook a complicated experiment in the regulation of human behavior.

All of these were fundamental and far reaching changes in the basic law of the land, and they were accompanied by many other alterations, some effected by interpretation, some by statute and some by common custom. Furthermore, sections of the Constitution have been ignored in what practically amounts to nullification in various areas of the nation. The electoral college as a means of electing the President has been overridden by the political parties; the Fifteenth Amendment has failed to give suffrage to the negro in great sections of the country; and the Eighteenth Amendment is patently ineffective in territories occupied by millions of our population.

In these instances the text of the document remains the same, but its spirit is gone. You may find the letter of the words, but not the life—the shell, but not the substance.

III. The truth, difficult for many to realize, is that a constitution does not consist of words alone but of public attitudes and habits. It is not a document alone, but a general understanding as to ways of doing things political. We deceive ourselves when we conclude that there is magic in the written word, apart from the situations of which it is a part. Words it is true, have their own peculiar symbolic power which must not be underestimated, but the symbolism itself is of little value if it is not representative of what is socially living and active. There is nothing so dead as a dead symbol, as any one may testify who sees some of the ancient monuments of departed glory in older lands where change has swept over the face of power and brought new authority with it. What power have the imperial emblems of Germany, of Austria, of Russia, except to irritate and alarm?

A distinguished judge announced about 1834 that the meaning of "due process of law" was now so fully established that fortunately no further discussion was necessary. But my colleague, Dr. Mott, recently wrote a 700 page volume on "due process" in the course of which he cited some 2,000 cases.* And he tells me that there are now many more decisions on "due process" each year than ever before.

We went to war in 1861 to save the Constitution, but within a short time President Lincoln declared that if necessary he would break the Constitution—to save the nation's life. Just as he might cut off a limb to save a life, he reasoned. And who can say, except a worshipper of forms and letters, that this was not a sound policy to pursue? Who would not

* Rodney L. Mott, *Due Process of Law.*

break the form to save the substance of the nation or of any other group?

IV. It is a common fallacy to believe that a written constitution is a bulwark of property and persons, of law and order, of fundamental justice. But those who thus rely upon the words of any constitution for such support are leaning upon a broken reed; and their sense of security is a false one. The Constitution does not protect persons and property against unjust invasion, or prevent governmental control and regulation of business, for after all this depends upon interpretation and application by courts and other governing authorities. And these agencies are selected from among mankind, filled with the spirit of the time in which they live.

Under the taxing power of Congress, it is possible to take most of a man's income, if desired, in a perfectly lawful way. Nor is there yet a limit to the use of the inheritance tax. Apparently the law of inheritance is not protected by the United States Constitution, and might be repealed by the several states. In this case the court might perhaps come to the rescue, but not yet, even in the face of the most drastic inheritance taxes.

The taxing power may even be invoked to destroy an industry, as was attempted unsuccessfully in the case of oleomargarine. The control over the United States mails may be employed to prohibit their use by a business and thus practically drive it from the competitive field. And the wide range of interstate commerce powers, even if narrowly interpreted, leaves enormous authority in the hands of the law-making bodies.

Government ownership and operation of railways is not prevented by the Constitution or the courts, but by the judgment of the majority of Congress and the president.

Nor can the court, even the Supreme Court, be regarded as a check upon invasion of alleged private rights. The number of judges may be fixed by Congress and additional appointments made by the president if in sympathy with Congress. This was actually done in the Legal Tender cases, where a national emergency seemed to justify saving legal tender money. The appellate jurisdiction of the higher courts may be altered and the establishment of new courts regulated by Congress.

All words may be interpreted, and the position and power of the Supreme Court does not depend upon the text of the Constitution but upon the general attitude of the people and their willingness to acquiesce in its decisions. If this should change radically, the whole attitude of the court would change, and all alleged guaranties with it. Mr. Dooley said, speaking of the decisions of the Supreme Court in the Insular cases, affecting American control over the Philippines, whether the United States Constitution follows the flag or not, the Supreme Court follows the election returns, referring to the triumphant election of McKinley on that issue, or when that issue was raised.

Imagine a Tammany president, a Tammany Senate made up of 96 sachems, a House of 435 braves, a Cabinet of ten Tammany men tried and true, a Supreme Court of nine Tammany adherents, and what would the Constitution be counted among friends?

Imagine a Socialist President, a Socialist Senate, a Socialist House, a Socialist Cabinet, and a Socialist Supreme Court, and what would be your guaranties against Socialism?

Imagine a Grundy President, a Grundy Senate, a Grundy House, a Grundy Cabinet, and a Grundy Supreme Court, and what would be your guaranties against what I suppose we may call, may we not, Grundyism, for lack of a better term?

A party or group electing a Congress and a President could completely control the courts and work its will through law and interpretation without legal check.

I make bold to say that "free institutions" rely in the last instance on the "general genius of the government." I undertake to say that "particular provisions, though not altogether useless, have far less virtue and efficacy than are commonly ascribed to them."

This you may perhaps regard as heretical—the language of an over-enthusiastic professor of political science. But in fact it is a quotation from Alexander Hamilton in the *Federalist,* Number 83.

The true guaranty of liberty lies not in parchment barriers, but in the fact that there is a common understanding the government shall be in the hands of agents who are responsible to the people, and who may displace them or overthrow them as they will.

It is true that the Constitution of the United States is more difficult to amend formally than other modern constitutions; and the constitutions of the several states themselves.

The requirement of a two-thirds' vote in each House and ratification by three-fourths of the states was intended to protect the small states against the others, but in modern times may play into the hands of another type of a minority. The case of the income tax is directly in point. The repeal of the Eighteenth Amendment would present grave difficulties even if a majority were so minded. Various plans for easier amendment have been presented, notably the device of Dean Burgess of Columbia School of Political Science in 1890.

"I cannot sympathize," says Burgess, "with that unreserved commendation of the fifth article of the Constitution of the United States indulged in by Mr. Justice Story and other commentators. When I reflect that, while our natural conditions and relations have been requiring a central government, not a single step has been taken in this direction through the process of amendment prescribed in that article, except as the result of civil war, I am bound to conclude that the organization of the sovereign power within the constitution has failed to accomplish the purpose for which it was constructed." [3]

The particular method suggested by Dean Burgess was as follows: "If, for example, the Congress should, in joint session and by simple majority, resolve upon a proposition of amendment, and give notice of the same to the people in time for the voters to take the matter into consideration in the election of the members of the House of Representatives for the

[3] Burgess, John W., *Political Science and Comparative Constitutional Law,* Vol. I, p. 150.

next succeeding Congress; and if the succeeding Congress should then repass the proposition in joint session and by like majority; and if then it should be sent to the legislatures of the commonwealths for ratification by the houses thereof, acting in joint assembly and resolving by simple majority vote; and if then the vote of each legislature should have the same weight in the count as that of the respective commonwealth in the election of the President of the United States, and an absolute majority of all the votes to which all of the commonwealths were entitled should be made necessary and sufficient for ratification—why would not this be an organization of the sovereign, of the state within the Constitution, which would be truthful to the conditions of our national democratic society and our federal system of government; which would secure all needful deliberation in procedure and maturity in resolution; which would permit changes when the natural conditions and relations of our state and society demanded them; and which would give us an organization of the state convenient in practice, and, at the same time, sufficiently distinct from the organization of the government to prevent confusion of thought in reference to the spheres and powers of the two organizations."[4]

It will be observed that this suggestion came, not from a radical, but from a conservative nationalist, concerned with the maintenance of the balance of power between numbers and amending authority.

It is true that this difficulty of formal amendment has from time to time in later

[4] Burgess, John W., *Political Science and Comparative Constitutional Law,* Vol. I, pp. 152-153.

years served to protect various vested property interests, but these paper barriers are in reality dependent on social and economic conditions for their force, and upon popular habit and acquiescence for their validity. When these supports fall away, the value of the words and the guaranties disappear with them. Experience shows further that if laws are made more difficult to amend than the social and political balance warrants, the result is not immobility but violence and sudden action in many instances. The community has many ways of dealing with laws it does not like, from quiet indifference, to open defiance, or to swift and retaliatory movements within or without legal bounds.

The basic reason for opposition to change is not the text of the Constitution, but the habits and attitudes of the

American people. The adoption of the Eighteenth and Nineteenth and the defeat of the Twentieth Amendment were great mass movements in which constitutional mechanism proved to be relatively unimportant. The War crisis made possible the Eighteenth Amendment; the War and the oncoming election of 1920, aided the Nineteenth; and the Twentieth fell before a sudden landslide quite unforeseen either by friend or foe.

V. The danger in American government at the present time is not *lack of stability, but lack of mobility,* failure to make prompt adjustments to the new era in industry and science. Government is at many points a generation behind the development of social and economic life and the urgent problem is that of bridging the gap. The large waste and misdirection of public funds, the failure to utilize scientific methods in government, the lack of forward looking plans on the part of responsible governing agencies; these are a part of the problem of America. And here we must think in terms of adaptation and adjustment rather than of immobility and equilibrium.

Our Constitution was born in revolution and the work of bold and experimental statesmen. It has been swept by a series of revolutions in many ways altering its original character, for the Fathers themselves provided for and expected change. Statesmanship of an equally bold and experimental type is needed in the present hour for the solution of the pressing problems of American public life.

We are emphasizing wealth, mechanics, science in America, but often without social or political vision, and without broad views of the trend of the time.

Imagination and invention are needed as well as enthusiasm and industry; sail as well as ballast. There was probably never a period in history when social change was as rapid as at present and when the need for adjustment and adaptation was as great. This is the spirit of business, the spirit of labor, the spirit of education, of professions, of religion even, and the governmental relations are no different from that of the community that produces them and in which they live.

Each generation makes a new spirit, a new constitution, a new way of doing things political, a new set of understanding as to what should be done for the common good by the government, and how. The notion that our government does not or should not change, is to a considerable extent responsible for the backward condition of our every day governmental institutions. Sometimes it seems as if, just because everything else changes rapidly in America, we try to hold our government unchangeable. So when the merit system in public employment is suggested, it is branded as un-American; the city manager form of government in cities is held to be un-American; consolidation of executive authority in cities is called un-American; and any change in national institutions is held to be un-American whether it is a world court or an income tax or a child labor law.

And folly of follies, to prevent change, we must in all too many places prevent protest and discussion. Free speech must be denied, free discussion of the bases of government prohibited, text-books must be censored in the interest of pseudo-patriotism; and the reign of intolerance must be invoked to prevent reflection upon the changeless and unchangeable political perfections of our time.

One might suppose from examining some types of legislation and some types of protests against text-books that the American system of government would collapse if all the truth were told about it, and that our only safety lay in the most rigid censorship of free discussion of the facts and the fundamentals of government.[5] Is it not a paradoxical situation that, in order to protect the Constitution, the guaranties respecting abridgment of the freedom of speech and the press, and the right of people peaceably to assemble and petition the government for a redress of grievances, are themselves assailed in periods of profound peace?

[5] See Bessie L. Pierce, *Public Opinion and the Teaching of History*.

There are great values in the past experience of men and of nations, and they must not be lost; but there are also great values in the forward look, in experiment, invention, in adaption and adjustment, especially in a swiftly moving nation like young and giant America.

The Constitution is not an idol but a spirit; not a form of words but a set of political attitudes and habits of behavior. Those who worship the text, worship in reality their own attitudes which they fondly hope the interpretation of the text may produce; or they clutch blindly at verbalisms whose real meaning they have never caught. The Spirit of America is the spirit of change and adjustment. I heartily commend to every citizen, Raymond Fosdick's recent volume on *The Old Savage in the New Civilization,* and if modesty did not forbid, I should refer to my own *New Aspects of Politics.*

States of mind are more important than the texts of constitutions, without detracting from their importance. The real difficulty lies in the unwillingness of many Americans to face in government what they meet in industry, the constant need for readjustment and reorganization. Social and industrial revolution on the one hand and governmental fossilization on the other, are another formula for new wine in old bottles. I am not unmindful of the fact that the government of cities is being profoundly transformed not only in form but in method; that some changes are being made in states; and that a new spirit is entering into national government and into our conception of our international relations. But government still lags, with its twelve billions of expenditure a year, its vast powers over persons and property, and its enormous potentialities for weal or woe in the industrial and social life of the community.

Finally, the wealth and power of America thrust us into a position, whether we wish it or not, of leadership in democracy and in world affairs. We cannot abdicate the position into which we have come, and we must make our contribution to the reorganization of government and the new politics of the new world into which we sweep. Nor, I take it, is there any real disposition to shirk this common responsibility, this opportunity for constructive effort in the domain of the political. Organization and efficiency have been developed in our industrial organization, and incredible as it may seem to some, it is not improbable that we may make like contributions to the operation of government, when once we strike our pace again. A new statesmanship is emerging in America, typified by Smith, the Tammany boy from under the bridge, by Lawyer Seasongood of Cincinnati, by Dwight Morrow and his new diplomacy, by Professor President Wilson. For these types are not accidents, but ride on the waves of a great trend toward another shore than that of spoils and graft and narrow partisanship.

II

NATION, STATE, AND CITY UNDER THE CONSTITUTION

WHEN the Fathers established the Constitution, nation and state were joint tenants of the throne, and cities were still in the making. The urban population of the United States in 1790 was under four per cent of the total and the largest city was the metropolis with a population of 42,000.

One of the greatest upturns in American political life is the triple movement seen in (1) the decline of the state, (2) the dominance of the nation, and (3) the emergence of the urban community. The great rivals for position and prestige are now the city and the state, while the position of the nation as supreme over both is uncontested.

How have these three rivals developed in their relations with and under the United States Constitution?

The greatest inventive achievement of the Fathers was the creation of a federal system of government in which the powers of the local and the national governments were so carefully balanced that neither could claim supremacy, except within its own sphere. And how the line should be drawn between competing jurisdictions, they were not careful to answer. Federalism was a triumph of diplomacy in a difficult field.

The dominance of the nation was not long in doubt, however. Andrew Jackson and John Marshall in their own characteristic ways thrust the state back and the nation forward. These individuals merely reflected the nationalizing trend of their time, which was sweeping the western world in the same general direction, whether in Germany, Italy, Switzerland, or the United States. Had it not been for a sharp difference in economic institutions, centering around slavery, the nationalizing process would in all probability have gone quietly on until it had done its perfect work. But the Civil War crisis was precipitated, and the work of Marshall and Jackson was completed on the field of battle with Grant and Lincoln as the spokesmen of the time. A generation of nationalistic interpretation of the United States Constitution has still further exalted the position of the central government and depressed that of the states, and the plunge of the United States into the stream of world affairs in

1898, and again in 1917, has added to the already overwhelming tendency toward nationalistic dominance.

It is the American flag that goes abroad and not that of a state. The President is first, not the Governor. At Washington the Supreme Court exalts the national interest. The Federal law is uniform while the concurrent action of forty-eight states is almost impossible to secure; and if they agree on the language of a uniform law, the forty-eight courts of the forty-eight states will interpret it differently as the Commission on Uniform Legislation has discovered to its sorrow—and wrath. The economic change from agriculture to industry, and in the business system to large-scale units of production, the rapid development of means of communication and transportation, the accompanying pressure for uniformity—all these factors make the rôle of the state increasingly difficult. Industrial and social developments do not follow state lines, and they tend to leave the state stranded with only historical tradition to maintain its life.

Seventeen states have a population of less than a million each; two states have a population equal to that of twenty others, with four senators against forty. In 1790 the highest ratio in state population was thirteen to one, Virginia and Delaware. Now it is one hundred thirty-four to one, in New York and Nevada.

If incomes are contrasted, the discrepancy becomes even wider. Three states pay practically one-half of the United States' income tax, New York, Illinois, and Pennsylvania (1929); and the ratio between the highest and the lowest state is over seven hundred to one.

Thirteen states paying an income tax of about $25,000,000 in a total of $2,331,-000,000 could block an amendment to the Constitution and they control twenty-six votes in the Senate.

Thirteen states with a population of 5,000,000 could block a Constitutional Amendment, against the will of the other 100,000,000 and would do so if geography and economic interests coincided. The Eighteenth Amendment illustrates some of the political problems encountered in such situations.

It is of course possible that such a lack of balance might continue for an indefinite period of time, but taking a forward look, it seems more probable that we shall face the task of readjusting the representation and position of the states in the federal union. The Constitution guarantees the equal suffrage of the states in the Senate, but does not stand in the way of the division of states, and the consent of the states themselves would make possible the variation of the equality now enjoyed in the upper branch of Congress.

In any such readjustment, it will be necessary to consider the emergent position of the modern city, and its demands for recognition in the political order of which it is so important a part. The growth of the city and especially the growth of the metropolitan region is one of the outstanding social phenomena of our time, and cannot be neglected in a study of the trends of national life.

A metropolitan district is defined by the United States Census Bureau as "the city proper and the urban portion of the territory lying within ten miles of the city limits." The census also takes account under another head of the whole region within ten miles, whether urban or not. In 1920 there were seven metropolitan regions each having a population of over a million and a total population of nineteen million. There were ten others each having a population of over five hundred thousand with a total of seven and one-half million. Together these comprise a total of seventeen regions each having a population of over five hundred thousand and a total population of twenty-six and one-half million. By way of comparison it may be pointed out that there are fifteen states of the American Union with a population of less than one million and nine states with a population of less than five hundred thousand.

Regions of the type of New York, Chicago, Boston, Philadelphia, like London, Paris, Berlin, are unities in the economic sense of the term and they also represent types of social and cultural unities. From the governmental point of view, however, their organization is highly decentralized. Each of these regions contains a large number of independent governments, often over-lapping and often conflicting and without any central administrative control or supervision. In the Chicago region, for example, which we construe as fifty miles from State and Madison streets, there are not less than 1,800 independent governing agencies undertaking to carry on the governmental functions incidental to the life of a community of something over four million people. Metropolitan Chicago extends into four different states, Illinois, Wisconsin, Indiana, and a corner of Michigan; it includes fifteen counties and an innumerable array of cities, villages, towns, townships, school districts, park districts, drainage districts. New York extends into three states, New York, New Jersey, and Connecticut, with a wide variety of county and local governments within her borders. There are already ten million people in the New York region and it is estimated, somewhat optimistically I suspect, that there will be twenty-five million in the New York area within another generation. It is conservatively estimated that the population of the Chicago area in 1950 will approach eight million. Problems of regional organization are presented not only in American cities such as Boston, Philadelphia, Pittsburgh, Cincinnati, San Francisco, but in the great cities all over the world.

The difficulties of urban development are still further accentuated by the fact that for half a century since the beginning of the modern urban movement, cities have been harshly treated by the states of which they were parts. They have been denied necessary powers of local self-government, or granted these powers only tardily, often at the hands of incompetent, partisan and corrupt legislatures.

In the United States we have experimented elaborately with various systems of so-called home rule for municipalities, hoping in this manner to free the urban center. These plans have often given some relief to cities, as in Ohio typically, but in general they have fallen far short of the mark at which they aimed. The courts have materially narrowed the range of local autonomy, as a rule, and thus often defeated the hopes of the cities. But even more serious has been the failure of the state to set up appropriate methods and instrumentalities for administrative supervision of municipal activities. The state has found difficulty in administering itself, to say nothing of the task of supervising the administration of its municipalities, and has been guilty of non-feasance at this point. Cities have usually had what is commonly called either a feast or a famine. Cities have been given too much power without supervision, or not enough with wise and temperate supervision. In any case it is too much to expect New York to supervise New York, or Illinois to supervise Chicago, when these cities are half of the supervising body itself.

Cities have been benevolently protected by constitutional and statutory restrictions against almost everything except deadlock and paralysis. There is today among the statutes of Illinois a measure giving specific authority to the city of Chicago to license the selling of peanuts and popcorn on the municipal pier, and the checking of hats and coats. States have the power of life and death over cities, but have not been willing to assume paternal responsibilities. If a state could be guilty of crime, some of them would long ago have been brought before some court of competent jurisdiction and punished, as are neglectful parents in a modern court.

Not only is this true, but cities have been refused adequate representation in the common councils of the state where the common policies of the commonwealth are determined. Most of the larger cities have been deliberately deprived of proportionate representation by a perfectly bare-faced denial of equality in representation. In Illinois, Chicago still has the same number of representatives in the legislature in 1930 as in 1900, and all the astounding growth in numbers and wealth during a period of thirty years counts for nothing, and that, too, in spite of a perfectly plain constitutional provision which is biennially nullified. At the same time we have one judge of the supreme court—in fact, only a part of one, in a total of seven.

Far be it from me to decry the virtues of the countryside. That they are numerous, substantial, and indispensable, we may hasten to concede. Whether they warrant a rural dictatorship over urban communities may be questioned, however. In fact, in my particular field at least, we know little about the specific differentials attributable to urban and rural environments and living conditions. It is easy to compare certain types of urban areas with certain other types of non-urban, but most of these assume that bad housing and poverty are essentially urban; and there are many other complicating factors into which it is impossible to enter here.

It is probable that in the near future there will be heard a strong plea for the organization of certain metropolitan regions as independent states. I venture to predict that some such experiment will be made in the next generation and for my part I should watch the trial with great interest. It would be interesting to observe the fortunes of the state of New York or New New York, or whatever name it might assume; or the state of Chicago; or the state of Philadelphia; or the state of Cincinnati. Such an experiment would give adequate scope for the development of metropolitan regional planning, including communication, transportation, housing; for the development of constructive recreational or leisure-time policies adapted to urban conditions; for the development of preventive as well as repressive police functions; for the expansion of the public welfare system appropriate to urban conditions; for the development of a metropolitan system of jurisprudence, differing from the now dominantly rural type.

The immediate pressure of urban situations, responsible control by an urbanized opinion, the presence of experts who are technically competent and experimentally inclined, the availability of adequate financial resources, constitute conditions favorable to the type of experiment indicated.

The question will promptly be raised:

are cities capable of governing themselves, and would they not be worse off as states than they now are as municipalities? Is the municipal population capable of discriminating between sound and unsound leaders and policies? Certainly there would be no guaranty of the political millennium, but there would be this advantage. Responsibility would be definitely fixed and the chief loser, if any, would be the city itself. There would be no twilight zone of responsibility except that between the city and nation, and the metropolitan area would go up or down with its own control over its own local institutions.

The truth is that the state itself is standing upon slippery ground as a political unit. Thirteen of our states have an historical background, but as Burgess pointed out thirty years ago, the others are the creatures of the surveyor's chain, with a few exceptions. Since the states risked all in a war with the nation over their alleged sovereignty and lost magnificently, they have gone steadily down the gentle slope. In the new German constitution, the states lost even more heavily than here. Most states do not now correspond to economic or social unities and their validity as units of organization and representation may be and has been seriously challenged. The nation and the city are vigorous organs, but the state is not comparatively. Certainly as guides and guardians of cities, the states might be very useful to cities as administrative superiors, but practically they have no such function as a rule and it does not seem probable they will in the near future, as far as metropolitan regions are concerned.

To make a city a state would not be as notable a promotion as it would have been in the days when state and nation were rivals for power and prestige. A city would not be obliged to climb far to go beyond a state. Already there are fifteen cities of a population of over five hundred thousand; nine states with less population than that. And if economic resources and cultural prestige are added to numbers, the contrast is far more striking.

One reason why experimentation may begin in America is that none of the eight urban communities of a million population is a capital city, the center of a national government, as is London, Paris, Berlin, Moscow, or Buenos Aires, Warsaw, Vienna. Our greatest cities are neither national capitals, nor as a rule are they even capitals of states. They do not have the custody of the safety and security of diplomatic, naval, military, parliamentary centers; and the immediate reason for keeping them under the thumb of a central government is absent. An American city formed in the likeness of a state would more nearly resemble Hamburg or Bremen in the German system.

Of course, the question may be raised as to whether the large urban aggregation is a desirable form of human association, and whether we ought not to use every effort to prevent the concentration of population upon limited areas. Perhaps we should strive for a garden-city type of aggregation and discourage the skyscraper city. All this may or may not be true, but the overwhelming tendency has been and continues to be in the direction of still greater concentration; and

I see no likelihood of any immediate change toward decentralization. In America the agricultural areas were almost ruined by the World War, and the recovery will be a slow one, while on every hand, the revolutionary tendencies of science are driving the ancient types of agricultural production farther and farther into the background. No one knows whether the farmer will become a chemist or the chemist a farmer.

Can the cities produce and utilize effective political leadership, and can they assume the guidance of our political destinies? A portentous question, this, for on the answer to it depends the future of America, the future of democracy and perhaps of Western civilization itself. There is eminent authority for the conclusion that cities are inherently inclined either toward tyranny on the one hand

and mob rule and demagoguery on the other, and many important illustrations might be found in support of this position. It might fairly be said that thus far, in the United States, cities have not produced their share of statesmen; but we are concerned not with where we are, so much as with where we are going, as we are with the trend or curve, the direction. There are striking examples of urban leaders in the person of Cleveland of Buffalo, and of Theodore Roosevelt of New York, not to speak of many contemporary figures in national life. If we were to consult the records of European statesmen, we should find the urban group strongly represented in the national gallery of statesmen, as in the case of Joseph Chamberlain, whose most enduring fame was attained as mayor of

Birmingham; or Herriot, mayor of Lyons.

In any event it is clear that the future United States will be dominantly urban. More than one-half our population is already in the cities, and the curve sweeps steadily upward in the same direction. In another generation, unless the rate or direction changes, two-thirds of the population of the United States will be urban. We may as well recognize now a situation to which many insist upon closing their eyes, namely, that the tendencies, the attitudes, the aptitudes, the political standards of America, will be predominantly and characteristically those of the cities in the near future. The combination of wealth, numbers, and prestige in the urban regions makes this inevitable. If these new urban groups really prove to be constitutionally incapable of self-government, America also will be incapable of self-government. Unless we suppose that political leadership is evolved from something else than the social, economic, and cultural material of which our society is made up—an illusion upon which many ideologies have been shattered.

The balance of power between central and local authority—a recurring problem in politics—might be aided by utilizing the weight of the urban communities against that of the central government; and cities would perhaps be more effective than states in maintaining the balance between center and circumference.

From another point of view, the administrative supervision of cities might be more effectively accomplished by the United States government than by the state of which cities are now parts. New York and Illinois are not strong enough to supervise New York City and Chicago, and the difficulty will be increasingly greater if the present trend of population continues. Minimum standards of police and health administration are admittedly desirable but unattainable under the system of voluntary cooperation or state supervision.

In a contest recently held by the Chicago Tribune for the remapping of the United States, there were some three thousand maps submitted from all over the country. The winning map provided for the retention of thirty-one old states, the creation of nine new states by consolidation, and the establishment of ten new city states—a total of fifty states.

One may say that it will prove extremely difficult to alter the established lines of the present states, and that nothing short of some great crisis can bring this about. This may well be, but it will prove just as difficult on the other hand to hold industrial influence and power within the outgrown lines of state organization. It will prove difficult to gerrymander public opinion, and hold it within the boundaries of state lines; or to retain propaganda and pressure groups within the boundaries of the older states. These influences will overflow any channel that may be cut for them, and where they cannot influence directly they will make themselves felt indirectly and circuitously. State lines alone will prove a feeble barrier against the trend of social and industrial forces, which are not in harmony with the ancient system. Such a situation as the maintenance of feeble lines, it must be observed, will, furthermore, weaken the force of representative institutions, and throw increasing emphasis on extra-legal forms of governmental consideration and determination, on groupism rather than on territorial divisions, and in this respect such a tendency may coincide with fundamental changes in our economic and political organization.

Our own Constitution overflowed the limits set by the earlier Articles of Confederation and found a broader channel of law and fact. And it cannot safely be presumed that the descendants of the Fathers will be less adventurous and enterprising than their ancestors, or less skillful in making new political patterns and fashions.

My conclusion is:

1. That it is necessary to face in the near future the reorganization of

state boundaries in such manner as to bring the lines of social and economic interest and power more nearly to those of the formal government.

2. That in this process the emergent city may, as seen in the great metropolitan regions, find a position among the commonwealth of states, experimentally at any rate.

3. That a coming topic of very great importance in the field of constitutional and administrative relations is that of the relative positions of the city and the nation.

III

THE CONSTITUTION AND POLITICAL PARTIES

CURIOUSLY enough from a present day point of view, the written Constitution of the United States contains no mention of political parties, important as they are in our political world. The framers did not contemplate the selection of Congressmen or President by permanent political organizations. The attitude of Washington in his Farewell Address on political parties is well known and was typical of the time—fear of the excesses of the partisan spirit and an apprehension that factionalism might in some way disintegrate the single-minded devotion of the patriot.

Later the powerful arguments of Calhoun and Webster regarding the dangers of the party system as it began to develop under Andrew Jackson, less well known in our time, were vigorous and impressive arraignments of the spoils system and its possibilities. Calhoun's prediction regarding the effect of the party system upon the interpretation of public law and the relations of the various parts of the government was especially forceful. The party system is not the creature of the original Constitution, although it sprang out of the generation that framed it, and put it in operation.

But we may inquire what are the relations between the Constitution and the parties as they now operate. What, if any, conditions and limitations are established by the Constitution affecting the problems and processes of the party?

What is likely to be the future relation of the party system to the constitutional order?

In the main, the party system has developed outside the range of direct constitutional provision and interpretation, by voluntary action of groups, and by common custom and consent. In the various states of the Union there is abundant legislation regarding the practices of political parties, determining the character of the nominating system and prescribing the organization and powers of party authorities. The national government, on the other hand, has had relatively little to do with statutory control over the party system. The United States has frequently exerted its prestige to bring public opinion to bear upon party practices, but seldom to regulate and prescribe them. For example, the Congressional inquiries into the subject of lobbying have been important, as in the Mulhall and other investigations. Various inquiries into the spoils system and into the workings of the merit system have thrown light upon the operations of party patronage. In the contests over the seating of members, notable revelations have been made, as in the Lorimer case, the Vare case, the Newberry case, the Smith case, to take only a few examples among many.

The Congressional limitations upon campaign expenditures have inevitably developed various aspects of the party system but the restrictions have been relatively ineffective. Indeed, one of the chief values of the laws has been the incidental revelations regarding their violation. In practice the exceptions have been so large, and the entanglement with local contests so close that it has been impossible to say how much has been expended for the Congressman and how much for the sheriff or ward committeeman. Even modern accountancy has its limitations.

Federal control over Federal elections is of course very comprehensive, but has seldom been exerted to its full extent. The period following the Civil War was an exception, but since the Federal troops were withdrawn from the polls in 1877 the authority of the United States government has not been exercised for this type of control. The so-called Force bill, reviving Federal control, died in the '90's and has not been revived since that time, even with the Republican Party in power and the possibility of rescuing the colored vote for the party.

Many new features of possible party

development are in no manner prevented by the Constitution as thus far interpreted. There is nothing constitutionally impossible about the adoption of the bloc system, if it were desired to establish such a type of political practice. It is quite conceivable that the representation in Congress might be split up among three or more parties in such a manner as to make group combinations the regular feature of our party life. From time to time such a division has temporarily been found in various periods of protest or ferment in party struggles, and there is no constitutional reason why such a situation might not continue indefinitely, if the political and social facts warranted it.

Nor is there anything to prevent the division of votes among several parties in the electoral college in such a manner as to develop party blocs for choice of President. These groups might engage in all sorts of preliminary bargainings and trades before the meeting of the electoral college, or in the House and Senate in case the college failed to elect the President and Vice-president respectively. Those who regard with alarm what they conceive to be the radical and dangerous character of party blocs find no special warrant in the Constitution for objection to such a plan. Thus far the American people have preferred the two party system and apparently are in a mood to continue in this practice; but if ever they wish to experiment with another form of party rule, the way is wide open to them, as far as the present Constitution is concerned.

Nor is there anything to prevent the adoption of a system of proportional representation on a large scale, if it were desired to do so. The individual states may determine the method of choosing presidential electors, and if they wish to set up a proportional system, there is nothing to prevent their doing so, as they may find it expedient. The single member district system for the choice of the lower house of Congress is the creation of a Federal statute which Congress might repeal at pleasure; and some other device might be substituted. This change requires statutory action only and involves no constitutional principle.

One of the most interesting phenomena of modern times is the development of various forms of highly organized groups, bringing pressure to bear upon governmental officials and in particular upon legislators. Child's study of the quasi-governmental activities of the

United States Chamber of Commerce and of the American Federation of Labor illustrates this [1]; Herring's study of representation before Congress [2] and Odegarde's on pressure groups [3] are of special value in this connection. Washington has in fact become a centre of competing groups, with their propagandas, their lobbies, their impressive headquarters; all becoming an integral part of the government of the land. The control of public opinion has become an art if not a science, and through organized agencies much of the public business of the nation is arranged and determined. There is, of course, no mention of propaganda or lobbies or pressure groups in the Constitu-

[1] H. S. Childs, *Labor and Capital in National Politics.*

[2] E. P. Herring, *Group Representation before Congress.*

[3] Peter Odegarde, *Pressure Politics.*

tion of the United States. Nor is there anything in the letter or the spirit of the Constitution to prevent their full and free functioning. In a sense they are modern developments of the right to assemble peaceably and petition for a redress of grievances. One might say that right of the freeman finds its equivalent in the present day privilege of bringing influence to bear more directly upon the public representatives.

If a combination capable of controlling all legislation was made between, let us say, the Chamber of Commerce, the Federation of Labor, the Farm Bureau, the National Educational Association, the American Legion, etc., and commands were habitually to emanate from their amalgamated or coordinated headquarters, there would be nothing in the Constitution to prevent their full and complete functioning through such majorities as they might be able to control. This would be merely a substitution of a group caucus for the traditional party caucus with which we have been familiar for these many years. I am not predicting such an outcome, but merely calling attention to the fact that it is perfectly possible without the disturbance of the existing constitutional text.

There are, however, points at which the general structure and framework of the Constitution and that of the party system do not articulate so well. Chief among these are:

(1) The requirement that no United States official shall at the same time be a member of the Congress.

(2) The requirement that the passage of a law demands the con-

currence of three elements, the two houses of Congress and the President.

(3) The requirement that the ratification of treaties shall be effected only by a two-thirds vote of the Senate.

(4) The apparent barrier to congressional regulation of party primaries.

(5) And above all, the Federal system itself.

1. The constitutional prohibition against membership in Congress simultaneously with office holding in the government was intended to safeguard the independence of the Congress from the possible intrusion and domination of the executive branch of the government. The founders feared the re-enactment on American soil of executive attempts to

control the parliament, and indeed must have recalled the struggles of the provincial governors to do likewise in the colonies. However, there is nothing to prevent the actual presence of cabinet members in Congress, or to bar their voice in the discussions of either house. Custom blocks the way here, and not constitutional requirement. If our party leaders were so minded, the setting up of such a system would present no difficulties of an insuperable nature. And conceivably the defeat of a cabinet measure might be followed by the resignation of one member or the entire cabinet and the executive, no matter for what term elected. I am not suggesting that this is either probable or desirable, but merely saying that there is nothing in the Constitution to stand in the way of such a practice and the evolution of such a system, if there were the will to achieve it.

2. More important is the requirement that the passage of a law shall have the concurrence of three elements, the two houses and the President. How often does it happen that the same party has all three points on its side? In the last fifty-two years the Democratic party has been in this position but eight years, and the Republican party for some twenty-four. During twenty years neither party had a majority large enough to enable it to carry through a consistent legislative policy in Washington. In the years '77-'89, '91-'93, '95-'97, '11-'13, '17-'19, no party was really in power. In such times important legislation must either be non-party or be reached by a series of compromises and concessions in which the parties and their factions are involved. It is not generally realized that for a

considerable part of the time no one is in a responsible position of power, and that the party system is almost suspended. It lives, on condition that it does not function. Theoretically, the minority party might yield to the party electing the President, or the presidential party might yield to the party coming fresh from the people in the congressional elections; but practically this does not occur, and in consequence there are long periods of time when no group is actually responsible for appropriations or for the legislative policy of the land. During twelve years of fifty-two, the President could not command a party majority of the Senate on the confirmation of presidential appointments.

3. Still more serious is the requirement that treaties must be ratified by a two-thirds vote of the senate. In the earlier

years of the Republic this was not so important, but when the United States became a world power with vast trade areas spread over the map, and with intimate relations with political and financial interests in a wide range of countries, the problem was more involved. During what percentage of the time during the last fifty years has one party been able to command a two-thirds vote of the United States Senate? The fact is that at no time has any one party been able to carry through a foreign policy requiring the ratification of a treaty for its fulfillment. If treaties are not partisan questions, then of course the issue is not raised; but if the issue does become a party matter then no one is in a position to act for the United States; neither the majority party nor the minority. As the phrase goes we declare war by a majority vote, but it takes two-thirds vote to conclude peace. At the end of the Spanish-American War, it would not have been possible to secure the vote necessary for ratification had not Mr. Bryan made a personal plea for the necessary democratic support, in order that hostilities might be ended, even though he personally opposed the particular settlement. At the end of the Great War, as every one knows, it was not possible to obtain action, either affirmative or negative, regarding the termination of the hostilities into which we had entered; and in the end it became necessary to conclude a separate peace with Germany. Our negotiations regarding the World Court have disclosed a similar situation, in which no one has the power to act, except negatively.

This constitutional relation with the

party system may well present difficulties of the most serious nature in the projection of American influence throughout the world in the generation just before us. It will tend to prevent parties from having a definite policy, even if they wish to do so; and it will weaken the position of our government in its dealings with the representatives of other governments. The question may well arise whether some other and less drastic provision than the two-thirds vote may not be necessary in the near future. The rise of presidential prerogative may be so great as to enable him to override the Senate, or there may be a modification of the two-thirds rule.

4. One of the most important elements in a party system is that of nominations for the various national offices. Could Congress provide by statute for a national

nominating system for these offices uniform in its detail and its operation and enforceable by federal authority? In the volume by Merriam and Overacker on *Presidential Primaries* this subject is fully discussed, and under the decision in the Newberry case, the passage of such a law is perhaps impossible even for Congress. It may be said that the exact meaning of this pronouncement of the Court, in view of the numerous and conflicting opinions rendered by the various justices, remains obscure. In any case only four of the justices clearly held that a primary is not an election, such as Congress may appropriately regulate, and until this interesting and important point is further illuminated by judicial finding, the whole situation must remain in doubt.

In the nomination of candidates for

President, it would be highly desirable to have a fixed day for the holding of primaries and a uniform method of procedure, and that without regard to whether the choice is to be made by delegates or directly. And the inconvenience of the present system may force the adoption of a uniform national system governing at least the general outlines of the procedure.

The method of constitutional amendment might well be employed for this purpose, if the statutory way is not open. The primary is fundamentally a part of the electoral process, and it seems inevitable that this will ultimately be recognized by the Federal authorities, after fuller discussion of the whole problem and of the significance of the nominating process in the American party system.

5. The Federal system itself makes dif-

ficult the establishment of parties capable of carrying through a policy. Authority is so divided between state and nation that in order to be really in power, a party must control not only the United States government but the government of each of the forty-eight states, to say nothing of numerous cities, counties, and other local governing bodies. And both state and national governments operate under many constitutional restrictions, as do cities under their charters. If a state is captured by a party it may appear that further Federal power is essential for the program and hence the party must go to Washington. Or if the national government is taken over, then it may appear that state authority is necessary for the plan and hence the party must move on to Albany, Harrisburg, Columbus, Lansing.

Dr. Harold F. Gosnell asserts that "The Federal system has hamstrung the party system." Professor Holcombe of Harvard is of like opinion in his brilliant volume on *Political Parties of Today*. The division of power, then, between the United States and the states works against the formation of powerful parties, and this division is intensified by the constitutional restrictions upon the ordinary government of state and nation. By the same logic, principles and policies become less important in parties, and patronage and spoils are relied upon to maintain the party spirit and activity.

Broadly speaking, we may say that the national stage has provided the setting for the party system, and has given it life and spirit, if soul would be too strong a word at this point. The states have supplied the detailed rules and regulations governing the process, although there are really no state parties in practice; the cities have done nothing to the development of a party system, and have tended to disintegrate and destroy it. The national party in the city usually has more machinery than soul.

It is indeed one of the surprising developments of our national history that although the parties owe their life and power to their national standing, the national government has allowed them to go on their way unmolested. There is to be sure no guaranty that this will continue and in fact many indications that this period of national indifference may come to a close, with the adoption of a more comprehensive regulative policy.

If we were to look ahead a little, the modern trends, if projected, seem to indicate:

1. There is a probability of national regulation of national party nominations.

2. There is little probability of a modification of the Constitution either by amendment or custom in such a fashion as to permit the adoption of a parliamentary system, in view of the fact that the trend is strongly in the direction of presidential government, with constant strengthening of the executive power.

3. The overwhelming trend in the direction of organized propaganda and lobbying is not inconsistent with any provision of the Constitution and will meet no opposition except from custom.

4. The increasing interest of the United States in foreign affairs may compel a reconsideration of the rule requiring a two-thirds vote for the ratification of treaties or the abandonment of foreign

leadership, the scientific ability which has produced modern civilization will fail to find solutions for these new problems the pessimist may aver, and may point out that thus far this has not been done, and that government lags behind modern progress. The optimist will look forward to a fruitful period of readaptation in which intelligence will be able to deal with the problems of ignorance and greed and evolve new and more beautiful forms of democratic cooperation.

It is, of course, easier to organize the hates and prejudices and greeds of mankind, to scatter the flames, to sow tares among the wheat while others sleep, to appeal to passion and prejudice than to organize human friendliness and the spirit of cooperation. But the history of modern civilization is the history of this slow process, and there is no reason to believe that the limit of human intelligence in cooperation has yet been reached, or very nearly approximated.

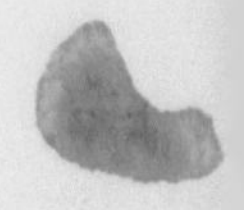